JAY'S T

1. Be Patient

2. **Don't Rush** ......You'll make mistakes.
3. **Don't Guess** ....You'll get into trouble.
4. **Don't Panic** .....It won't help.
5. **Don't Click** ......Until the mouse pointer is in the correct position.
6. **Don't Continue.** When you're stuck; think about what you just did.
7. **Always Save** ...Every 5 minutes and know where you are saving to.
8. **Always Know** ..The results of commands before executing them.
9. **Always Use** ....Computer terminology, it reinforces the learning curve.
10. **Always Locate.** The cursor before you make changes in your document.

FOR SUCCESS WITH THE COMPUTER™

JAY'S TEN COMMANDMENTS

1. Be Patient

2. Don't Rush ...
3. Don't Guess
4. Don't Panic
5. Don't Click ...

6. Don't Continue ...

7. Always Save ...

8. Always Know ...

9. Always Use ...

10. Always Locate ...

FOR SUCCESS WITH THE COMPUTER™

Introduction to PC & Windows
Basics for Beginners

Javad Saffarzadeh, M.S., M.A.

Information in this document is subject to change without notice.
No part of this manual may be reproduced or transmitted in
any form, by any means whatsoever, without the
written permission of Javad Saffarzadeh.

JS Computer Center, Inc.
724 Elm Street
Winnetka, Illinois 60093
Phone: (847) 501-2677
Fax: (847) 501-5638
E-mail: Jay@jslearning.com

Comments and questions are most welcome.

Edited by
Jim Grubman

This book is fondly dedicated to my students, all of whom have
been the inspiration for this work. They have shared the
unique gift of themselves with me; it is through
this sharing process that my teaching grows.

Author Acknowledgements

Special thanks go to the following people: Susan De Longis, M.P.S., for initially editing the manuscript and for motivating me to finish the work; Jim Grubman, whose hard work at editing this new version of the text improved it further; Denise Morette, for her contribution of the book cover designs; and Norwin Merens, for his marketing, public relations, and proofreading support. Finally, I would like to thank my dear wife for her endless patience; without her support, writing this book would have been impossible.

April 2000
Chicago, Illinois

About this Book

This book was written for those who need a clear and effective approach to the basics of computer learning. The language is intentionally aimed at the beginner. Concepts and procedures are presented in a logical, simple manner. Years of proven success in the classroom form the foundation of the techniques offered here. Many beginners face fear and frustration when they enter the world of computers. The author makes the journey both comfortable and exciting.

TABLE OF CONTENTS

Section 1
Terminology

Basic Computer Components

Figure 1 shows all of the basic computer components described below.

Figure 1

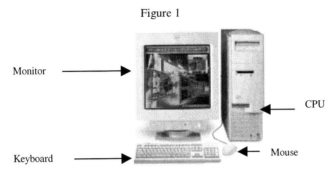

Monitor
The monitor is the screen that displays information contained in your computer. The monitor does not do any calculations.

Keyboard
The keyboard is the device that you use to enter information or commands into the computer. You communicate with your computer through the keyboard, and you then see the computer's response on your monitor screen.

Central Processing Unit
The Central Processing Unit (CPU) is the actual computer itself. It houses the computer's memory. The CPU does all the work of the computer. Desktop computer CPUs are either large, flat boxes on top of which many people place their monitors, or vertical towers that can sit on a surface next to the monitor or on the floor. Laptop computer CPUs are located underneath the keyboard.

Mouse

The mouse is a small plastic device that fits in the hand of the computer user and allows the operator—by moving it around on a mouse pad—to move the mouse pointer that is seen on the monitor screen. The pointer is used to select various options in a computer's programs.

Modem

External
Modem

A modem is a device that connects your computer to other computers through a telephone line. The actual function of the modem is to convert computer signals, which are digital, to voice signals, which are analog. Through the use of a modem, you can connect a normal telephone line to your computer. When the computer signals convert to voice signals, we have **mod**ulation. When those voice signals are converted back to computer signals on the other end, we have **dem**odulation. Putting the first part of the two words together, we have the word **modem.** The speed of a modem is very important, as it determines how quickly a modem can send or receive information. For example, today's modems should run at 56K. (We will explain this in more detail later.) A modem can be installed inside the computer or attached to it externally. Most of today's computers have internal modems.

Printer

Inkjet Printer

The printer prints out information from the computer. Although there are several criteria that determine the quality of a printer, the two most important features to consider are printer resolution and speed.

Printer Resolution: Resolution describes how many dots-per-inch (dpi) a printer can print. The more dots, the better resolution print you will have. For example, most printers today print 300 x 300 dpi–1200 x 1600 dpi, although this can go higher. A printer with a 1440 x 720 dpi resolution has a photo-quality capacity and can be used to print pictures.

Printer Speed: Older printer speeds were measured in characters-per-second (cps). Today, printer speed is measured in pages-per-minute (ppm). Some color printers have two speeds: one for color printing, and another for black-and-white printing, which is faster. For example, if a printer has a speed of 8 ppm for black and white, the speed for color printing will normally be less than 8 ppm.

Different Types of Printers

Dot Matrix: This is an older series of printers that works just like a typewriter. It uses ribbons, prints with dots, and its speed is measured in characters-per-second (cps).

Ink Jet: This is the most popular type of printer, especially for individuals and smaller businesses. It prints in color and offers high-resolution quality. Ink jet printers are relatively inexpensive.

Laser: This type of printer—used by individuals and larger businesses—has the best resolution, because it uses ink powder to print. Laser printers are made for either color or black-and-white printing. Color laser printers are very expensive compared to ink jet printers and are typically used for large-scale color publications.

Scanner

 A scanner is just like a copy machine, but it sends the copied images to a computer instead of onto paper. For example, when you scan a magazine article, the scanner takes a picture of the article and electronically sends it to the computer, where it can be stored. Although you cannot modify or change the text of this article with an older scanner, most of today's models come with a software program that allows you to convert a scanned picture of text to editable text that can be modified.

This feature is called Optical Character Recognition (OCR). The scanner's resolution, speed and extra options will determine its quality and price. Scanners are an excellent addition to your computer system, because they are competitively priced and easy to use.

Hardware & Software

Hardware (Equipment)
In the world of computers, anything you can physically touch (e.g., the monitor, printer, or keyboard) is called hardware. (In other words, hardware refers to all of the visible equipment.)

Software (Programs)
Software refers to the computer's programs. These are the instructions that make your computer work, and they are installed on the hard drive of your computer. This process will be discussed in greater detail later on.

Programs

A **program** is a group of coded instructions that tells a computer how to work. Any computer without a program is worthless. There are three types of computer programs: operating system, program language, and program application.

Operating System
In order for the computer to work, it must have an operating system program. The operating system controls the omputer's workflow, manages its files, and runs its functions overall. No computer can function without an operating system. Examples of current operating systems include Windows 98$^®$ or Windows 2000$^®$ for IBM and compatible computers, and Mac OS$^®$ for Macintosh$^®$ computers

Program Languages

These are the languages that computer programmers use to create program applications. Examples of program languages include Pascal™, Cobal®, C++®, and Basic®.

Program Applications

These are the programs that computer operators use to create files or documents. There are many different types of program applications, all used for different purposes. Following are some examples:

Word Processing Applications

A word processor's major function is to perform tasks that are usually produced with a typewriter, but with much more ease and speed. One of the main advantages of using a word processor is that it gives you the ability to create a document on the computer and put it aside. That way, you can edit it later, adding margin changes and paragraph indents, checking grammar and word spelling, and much more. You can even replicate the document many times, making small changes in each version. Current popular word processing programs include Microsoft Word® and WordPerfect®.

Spreadsheet Applications

A spreadsheet program is exactly like the old general ledger books that accountants once used; these contained many sheets, and each sheet had many rows and columns for entering numbers and making calculations.

A spreadsheet program's major purpose is to aid in manipulating and calculating numbers. It may be used to create an income statement, balance sheet, or petty cash itemization—that is, any list with a total. Once the calculations are in place, changing any calculation or entered

number automatically recalculates the total. This can save the user minutes or hours of time formerly needed to re-add the list. Spreadsheet programs also allow you to easily convert data into several types of graphs. Microsoft Excel® and Lotus 1,2,3® are examples of complete spreadsheet programs.

Database Applications
The word "data" means "information," so a database is a program that is based on information. To understand a database program, think of having a rotating card file like a Rolodex® on your desk. What is the purpose of a Rolodex? It is used to organize information such as names, phone numbers, addresses, etc. Once the information is sorted, it is easy to find.

A database program in a computer has the same function, but does much more. Microsoft Access®, dBASE®, and File Maker Pro® are popular database programs, but many businesses use predesigned database programs. Such programs can be customized for those who work in industries such as real estate, banking, health care, and any other industries or settings that use inventories. For example, when you call the telephone company and give them your name, they can find information for your name because it exists in their database program.

Desktop Publishing
This application combines graphics and text to create brochures, flyers, greeting cards, and even books. Examples of desktop publishing programs include Microsoft Publisher® and PrintShop®, which is used primarily in home systems. PageMaker® and Quark Express® are more popular for business use.

Program Versions

The first time that any program is marketed, it is called Version 1. Anytime it is upgraded, the number of the version is changed. If the upgrade is minor, the version number will be changed only slightly (e.g., to version 1.1 or 1.2). If major changes are made, the upgrade will <u>advance to a higher number</u> (e.g., Version 2 or Version 3). For example, Windows 95 is really Windows Version 4, because the previous version of Windows was 3.1. Windows 95 is just a name used to make it easier to understand how old or new the program is. Windows 98 is actually Version 4.1, so we know there is not much difference between Windows 95 and Windows 98.

It is important to know <u>which version of your computer program you have</u>. One of the main reasons for this concerns **file compatibility.** If you create a file in a higher version of Microsoft Word and then e-mail that file to someone who has a lower version of Microsoft Word, that person will not be able to open the file.

Note: There are many different kinds of software on the market, but the software programs described above are the most common ones.

Comparing Personal Computers

There are many factors that determine the performance of a **personal computer (PC).** The three most important factors to know (and that make a big difference in a computer's performance) are the PC's **processor, memory,** and **speed.**

Computer Processor

The processor (CPU) is the brain, or central control, of the computer—just as the human brain is for us. Compared with other parts of the computer, it is small, but powerful. It controls all of the computer's activities, and commands all other computer components. At the beginning of the book, we talked about the monitor, the keyboard, and the CPU (which actually refers to the little processor chip contained within the CPU box). This chip determines the performance and the speed of your computer. One of the largest manufacturers of the processor chip is Intel®.

Memory

"Memory" means the same thing as "space." Just as we use units of measurement (e.g., inches, liters, miles) to measure any kind of space, we need a unit to determine the size of a computer's memory. This unit of measurement is called a **byte.** One byte measures the amount of memory of one written character (e.g., a number, letter, punctuation mark, or even a space between words). To imagine how computer memory looks, think of a sheet of paper divided into many small squares, with each square representing one byte. In each square you can write a letter or number, or leave a space. Therefore, each byte can hold one character.

a	b	c	?	. .
4				

If someone asks you how large a piece of property you own, you probably are not going to say "2,350,455 square inches." You would more likely say "2 acres," since this is much easier to say. Why is it easier? Because we have an agreement with each other to call 12 inches a foot, 3 feet a yard, and so on. We have the exact same situation when measuring memory in a computer. However, computer bytes are measured in increments of 1,000, as follows:

1,000 Bytes   **= 1 KB (Kilobyte)**
1,000 KB   **= 1 MB (Megabyte)**
1,000 MB   **= 1 GB (Gigabyte)**

Note: When referring to memory size, we move up in increments of 1,000. As the amount of memory exceeds 1,000 units, we move up to the next level of measurement. So, instead of saying "2,000 KB" we say "2 MB," and instead of "4,000 MB" we say "4 GB."

To have some idea of how many bytes or kilobytes we need for a one-page document of simple text, solve this problem:

Assume that you have 10,000 bytes of memory in your computer, and you need to type a 10-page document.

Given
On 1 page you can type 60 lines.
On 1 line you can type 80 characters or letters.

Solution
Multiply 80 x 60 = 4800 bytes or **approximately 5 KB. Therefore, you need approximately 5 KB for a 1-page document.**

If you type ten pages, 5 x 10 = 50 KB or 50,000 bytes. Although 10,000 bytes sounds like a lot, it is not even enough memory to hold a 10-page document.

This information is handy to know, because it helps us to understand the meaning of the file size that a computer refers to when it tells us how many bytes a file contains. How would we know, for example, how big a 7K document is? Or, if we check a floppy disk's memory capacity and see that we have 2K of space left, how would we know whether or not this is enough space to hold what we want to save on the disk?

The above figures apply to documents that contain plain text. For documents containing graphic images, much more memory space is required. The purpose of using this calculation is to help in understanding the KB or MB designations that are so common in computer language.

Temporary Memory and Permanent Memory

In the computer, there are two types of memory: **working memory,** which is temporary, and **storage memory,** which is permanent. The following analogy can help us to understand the functions of these two types of memory.

Imagine you are sitting at your desk, and you want to type a letter to your insurance company. What do you do? You put the typewriter on your desk, if it is not already there. You put a blank piece of paper into the typewriter and you start to type. When you have finished typing, you send one copy to the insurance company and you make a second copy of what you have typed for yourself. You save your copy in your insurance folder, which is located inside your file cabinet. That is exactly the same way your computer works.

As you work on your document, you are using the **temporary space** available on the top of your desk. When you place a copy into the file cabinet, you are using permanent storage space. The computer also has two different uses of space, temporary and permanent. The space in which you temporarily to work on documents is called **RAM** (**R**andom **A**ccess Memory). This is like the top of your desk, and is only available when the computer is turned on. As soon as you turn off the computer, this memory is gone, just as if you had left your desk and were no longer using the space.

The permanent use of the computer's space is called **storage.** This works like your file cabinet, as a place to store your documents in folders. This storage space is held on either a **hard, floppy,** or **CD ROM disk.** In the next few pages, we will describe in detail the functions of the various types of storage.

Let's summarize: First, you used your computer to create a letter, called a **file**. You did this in your temporary, working space, called RAM. And, you saved your document in permanent storage on a disk. When you are working in RAM space, which is interchangeably called "memory," your document is available only while you are working on it. Once you have saved it to storage, the document will remain there permanently unless you decide to delete it.

How RAM Works

 RAM is a memory chip that holds information in a virtual way. In other words, it is not like hard or floppy disks, which are places that physically hold data. This is why you lose all of the data you had on RAM when you turn off your computer (unless, as mentioned, you first saved it to a permanent storage location).

Here's how RAM works: When you double-click on any program icon (i.e., the on-screen graphic image that represents a file, folder, or program) the computer makes a working copy of the program located on your hard disk and brings it onto your RAM. This allows you to see the program on your screen and work on it. When you type or create anything in that program, your file stays on your RAM. Once you saved it, you send a copy of whatever you have created on your RAM to the hard or floppy disk.

Now, going back to our analogy, the size of the desktop that you work on is very important. If your desktop space is not big enough, you may not be able to work with the materials you need from your file cabinet, or you may not be able to move them around easily. This concept also applies to the computer. The average size of RAM for today's computer is between 64–128 MB, but it can go much higher. The more RAM your computer has, the faster it can work with multiple applications or graphic programs.

Hard Drive

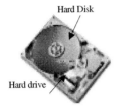

Hard Disk

Hard drive

As you can see in this illustration of an open **hard drive,** a hard disk is built right into the hard drive. Therefore, the terms hard disk and hard drive both refer to the same thing. Your hard disk is the place that holds all your computer's programs, files, and anything else that has been installed or saved in your computer. The memory capacity of your hard drive is very big. The average size for today's computer should not be less than 8 GB. When purchasing a new computer, it is important to get the largest hard drive you can afford, because, unlike RAM, the size of the hard drive is harder to increase later.

Note: Normally, the best laptop computers have less memory capacity and power than do the best desktop computers.

Floppy Drive

There are two types of floppy disks that can be inserted into the floppy drive: the older 5.25-inch disk, which is not typically seen in today's computers, and the standard 3.5-inch floppy disk. The 3.5-inch disk is available in high-density or low-density format. **Density** refers to the amount of data that the disk can hold. As shown in Figure 4 (on page 22), high-density disks can hold twice as much data as low-density ones. All of today's computers can use high-density disks. To determine the density of a disk, check the bottom of the disk (i.e., the non-notched one): if it has two holes, it is high-density; if there is only one hole, the disk is low-density. *(See Figure 2.)*

Inserting a Floppy Disk Into the Floppy Drive

The arrow on a floppy disk indicates the direction in which it should be inserted into the computer. *(See illustration below.)*

Figure 2

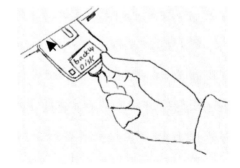

Write Protect Error

On both low-density and high-density floppy disks, there is a hole that can be closed or opened by moving the little plastic piece that covers it; this can be done with any small, pointed object. *(See Figure 3.)* If you open the hole, the disk is locked and you cannot save any new information on it. The information on the disk is then in the **write-protect** mode, and cannot be erased or changed. If you try to save any information on the disk while it is locked, the computer will give you the error message, "Write Protect Error." To work on the disk, you must take the floppy disk out and close the hole; this can be done with your fingernail or the tip of a pen.

Note: All floppy disks should be kept at least 6 inches away from any magnetic field (e.g., telephone, television, radio) to prevent the accidental erasure of information.

Figure 3

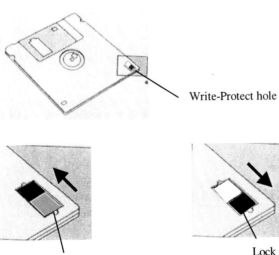

Write-Protect hole

Unlock

Lock

Zip Drive

Zip drives—which are also 3.5" inches in size—have the same function as floppy drives. The difference is in storage capacity. One zip drive can hold 100 MB or 250 MB; floppy disks, on the other hand, can hold up to 1.44 MB.

Figure 4

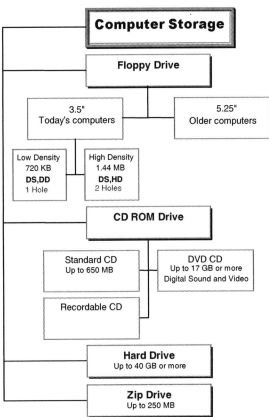

CD ROM, DVD, and Recordable CD Drives

 CDs (i.e., Compaq Disks) are popular due to their huge storage capacity. Information on more than 400 high-density floppy disks can be held on one CD, so most of today's software programs are offered on CDs. There are two different types of CDs: ROM (Read Only Memory), and recordable.

CD ROMs can only be read and played (i.e., you cannot add to, erase, or modify the information on the disk). The two ROM types include **standard** and **DVD (Digital Versatile Disk)**. The DVD drive is just like a CD ROM drive, but can hold up to 17 GB of storage, a far greater capacity than the regular CD ROM. This capacity allows entire movies to be loaded onto a DVD disk; these disks have digital sound and video, which is much clearer than standard CD ROM sound and video.

The second, more recent, type of CDs are **recordable CDs.** Recordable CDs allow you to create, save, and delete information just as you can with floppy disks, so they offer a great way to back up a huge amount of data on one CD; also, people who create music can record a song or any kind of music on one CD disk.

Computer Speed

The speed of your computer is an important issue, particularly when you are retrieving, processing, or copying a large program or file. These functions will be affected by the speed of many components within the computer, such as the RAM, hard drive, and motherboard (i.e., the board upon which all of the computer's internal components are placed). Speed actually refers to the time it takes to access and process data. However, the processor, or CPU, controls every function of the computer. So, the speed of the computer primarily refers to the speed of the processor, which is measured in Mega Hertz (MHz).

Hertz was the name of the German physicist who discovered the cycle of electronic signals. **One Hertz (Hz) equals one cycle-per-second.** The Hertz is a standard speed measurement that is used for many electronic devices. For example, a clothes dryer probably works at about 50 Hz. Radio stations function at around 75 Kilo Hertz (KHz). (Note that 1,000 Hertz = 1 Kilo Hertz.) However, the speed of a computer is much faster than this, and is generally measured in Mega Hertz (MHz). (Note that 1,000 Kz = 1 MHz.) Early computers had speeds starting at 4.77 MHz. Today's computers process at an average speed of 400 MHz, and can exceed 1 Giga Hertz (GHz). (Note that 1,000 MHz = 1 GHz.) When buying a computer, you will usually choose a processor speed of 450–600 MHz or more. Of course, you should purchase the fastest-speed computer you can afford, since this will directly affect your working time on the computer. The table on page 25 shows the history of the PC's development in terms of memory size and speed.

PC Categories Table

Microprocessor or CPU (Central Processing Unit)	RAM or Memory	Speed Range
PC 8086	64KB 128 KB 256 KB	4.77 MHz 6 MHz
PC XT (Extension of PC) 8088	512 KB 640 KB	8 MHz 10 MHz
PC AT (Advances Technology) 80286 80386SX 80386DX 80486DX 80486DX2	1 MB 2 MB 4MB 8 MB 10 MB 16 MB 32MB 64MB	12MHz 200
Pentium = 586 Pentium II = 686 Pentium III =786	128 MB & greater	266, 300, 333, 350, 400, 450, 500, 550, 600, 650 800 MHz & greater

Section 2
Getting Started

Before You Turn On Your Computer

Sitting In Front of the Computer

Sitting in front of your computer is like sitting behind the wheel of your car. It's important that you sit in the correct position. To help with this, you should have a good chair with strong back support. Your eyes should be level with the screen of your monitor. If the monitor is too high or is at a right or left angle to your direct vision, you're likely to get neck problems. Your arms should be at a 90-degree angle, and your forearms and hands should extend in a straight line toward the keyboard. If the keyboard is too high, you might end up with a painful condition in your wrists or hand. *(See Figure 5.)*

Figure 5

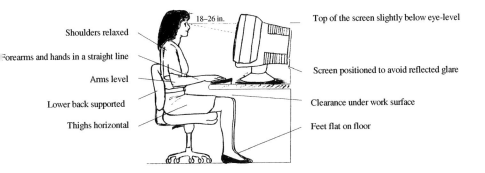

Shoulders relaxed	18–26 in.
Forearms and hands in a straight line	Top of the screen slightly below eye-level
Arms level	Screen positioned to avoid reflected glare
Lower back supported	Clearance under work surface
Thighs horizontal	Feet flat on floor

Using the Mouse Correctly

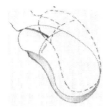 When you use the computer **mouse,** you're really just rolling the ball located inside the mouse casing. The wrist should remain steady while you lift and drag the mouse. This lifting action allows you to move the pointer all over the screen while using a very small amount of space on the mouse pad. With this technique, you avoid the frustration of feeling like your hand is running off the mouse pad or getting stuck.

When you use the mouse, your hand should gently rest over the casing. To click a button of the mouse, you hold the mouse firmly, but click lightly. It takes practice to develop a fast and light touch with your finger, while holding the mouse securely in your hand. A **double-click** must be very quick and light. Make sure that your hand does not move while you click, or it will not work.

Generally, the mouse's **left button** is used to open an icon, folder, or file (with a double-click), or to select an option (with a single click). What is the mouse's **right button** for? The right button always gives you an on-screen **drop-down menu** that offers certain options related to the icon that you have clicked on. (Note that all mouse-clicking instructions given in this book refer to using the mouse's left button unless otherwise stated.)

Single click or double-click? A **single click** is used to <u>select</u> an icon or option from a menu. A **double-click** is used to <u>open</u> an icon. This can be a file, folder, or program icon. In other words, using a double-click creates a new window. When double-clicking, always click on the icon, not on the name.

Using the Keyboard

The keys of your keyboard must be pressed very lightly or they will automatically repeat the letter or number of the key. For example, if you hold down the letter "a," you will end up with a row of a's. The exceptions to this are certain commands that require you to hold a key down, for example, the **Ctrl, Alt,** or **Shift keys.**

Using The Computer

Turning on the Computer

On a desktop computer model, both your CPU and monitor will have on/off buttons, usually located at the front or side of the unit. It does not matter which one you turn on first. A laptop will have just one button.

What is the Desktop?

Once your computer has opened the Windows program**, the first screen you will see is called the Desktop**. Each computer's desktop will have its own color and design.

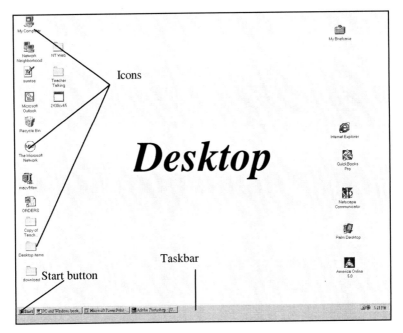

Elements of the Desktop

The following elements, identified in the illustration above, comprise the Desktop.

Icons

Icons are graphic symbols, with their names given under a picture. Each has its own special purpose. For example, you will find the My Computer icon on your desktop.

You will also see the icon for your **Recycle Bin.** The desktop will often display icons for the programs that have been installed (e.g., Microsoft Word) as well as any files or folders that have been saved onto the desktop.

Start Button

Normally, the **Start button** is located at the bottom-left of your desktop screen. Clicking on the Start button will bring up a menu with which you can access anything on your hard drive. You will notice that some of the options on this menu have small arrows off to the right side. Those options have sub-menus under them that might provide further selections by clicking on them.

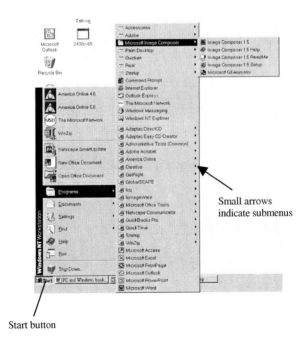

Small arrows indicate submenus

Start button

If you move the mouse pointer over an arrow, the computer displays the sub-menu. To select a sub-menu option, move your mouse pointer straight across to the sub-menu and click on your desired option. When moving your mouse, try to keep it in the middle of the highlighted area. If it is not in the highlighted area or your pointer is too far to the right or left side of the sub-menu, you will lose the sub-menu, and you will have to begin again.

Taskbar
To the immediate right of the Start button, you will see the **Taskbar.** The main function of the Taskbar is to display a button for any window you have opened.

Taskbar

Accessing The Hard Drive, Floppy Drive, And CD ROM Drive

How can you access your computer's different drives? They can be accessed through the My Computer icon located on your desktop. To do this, position the mouse pointer over the My Computer icon and double-click to open it. A window picturing several icons will appear; each drive has its own name and icon. (If you do not see a new window, it means that you moved your mouse while clicking; simply try again.) Next, double-click on the drive you want to open; the window that appears will show the contents of that drive. (For the floppy or CD ROM drives, you must insert your disk before performing these steps.) The letters below identify the drives:

A: Floppy drive
B: Second floppy drive (usually in older computers)
C: Hard drive
D: Zip drive or CD ROM drive (If your computer has more than one hard drive, the second one will be called the D: drive. Your CD ROM or Zip drive usually takes the next letter after your hard drive.)

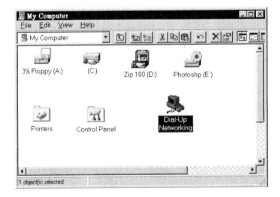

Note: If your computer is part of a network of computers, you will see a letter for each drive in the network.

Using CD ROM Disks

1. To open the drive, press the button located on the right side of the CD ROM drive.

2. Hold your CD with your thumb and forefinger so that you **touch only its sides.**

3. Gently place the disk into the drive and make sure it is **completely settled** into the recessed circle. (If the disk is not properly placed, it can damage the disk, the drive, or both when you try to close the drive.)

4. To **close the drive**, press the same button that you used to open it.

Working With Multiple Windows On The Screen

When you double-click on any icon, you are creating a window, and, of course, a window is something you can see through. If you double-click on a folder icon, the computer creates a window for that folder so that you can see what's in it. If you double-click on a file icon, the computer will create a window that allows you to see that file's contents. Also, if you double-click on a program icon, a window will be created to let you work in that program.

All open windows have certain elements in common that make it possible to manipulate one window or to work with several on your screen at one time. A window can be moved, resized, maximized, or minimized on the screen. Before we explain how to do these things, let's become familiar with the different elements of any open window on your screen or desktop.

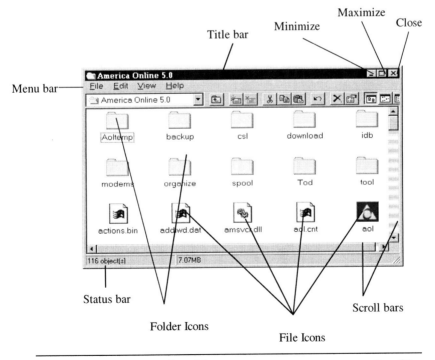

Title bar

The structure of a window is a box-shape with a **title bar** going across the very top. The title bar gives you the name of the window. If you have more than one window open on the screen, the active window will have a title bar that is colored differently from the other windows and be in front of the others. To activate another window on your screen, place your mouse pointer anywhere on that window and click once. That window will be brought to the front so you can work on it, and its title bar will now be in color, while the other windows' title bars will be a different color. If the window is underneath other windows and is not visible, you can locate it on the taskbar and click on it to activate it.

Menu bar

Just under the title bar is the **menu bar,** which offers several basic command options (e.g., File, Edit). You can find all the features of any program by using the Menu bar. When you click your mouse pointer on any of the menu bar commands, you will be shown a **drop-down menu** of functions. Drag the pointer down the list and click once to select any function.

Status bar

At the very bottom of any window you will see the **status bar.** This tells you how many objects are in the window and the total memory size of all files contained there. If you select a file by clicking on it once, the status bar will change to tell you the memory size of that particular file.

Minimizing, Maximizing, and Closing Windows

The three small icons at the right edge of the title bar are used for the close, maximize, and minimize functions.

Close

One click of the mouse button on the **Close icon** will completely close that window. When you do this, you will no longer see that window's name on the Taskbar.

Maximize

One click on the **Maximize icon** will make the window the full size of your entire monitor screen. When you maximize a window, other windows that are open on-screen will be hidden beneath it. To access a hidden window, just click on its name on the Taskbar as described earlier.

Restore

When you maximize your window, the Maximize icon will change in its appearance to the **Restore icon.** To restore a window to its original size, click once more on the Restore icon.

Minimize

Finally, you will see the **Minimize icon.** This name is confusing, because it sounds like it has something to do with the size of the window. This is not the case. A click on the Minimize icon will completely remove the window from the screen, but it remains open and can be found on the taskbar. To restore a minimized window to its original size, simply click on its name in the taskbar.

Note: As a beginner, it is important to practice these three functions to become comfortable with them, because you will use them often.

Moving Windows

Moving a window to another location on the screen is very simple. Position your mouse pointer inside the title bar, click and hold down the mouse button. Then, drag the window to the location you want it to be on the screen. Let go of the button when you are finished. *(See Figure 6.)*

Figure 6

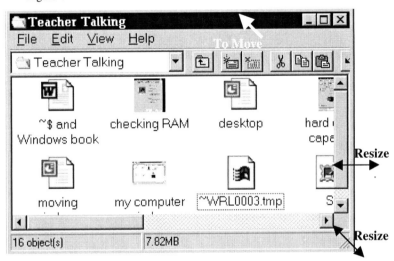

Resizing Windows

It is easy to change the size of a window. Slowly move your mouse pointer along the very edge of any side of the window, and you will see the pointer change to a double-arrow. When it does, click and hold down the mouse button. Drag the window sides until the window is your desired size and release the button. Using the double-arrow at the bottom-right corner of the window will allow you to adjust the bottom and right sides of the window at the same time. Using these two techniques, you can "shape" any window to get it smaller, larger, longer, or wider.

Scroll Bar

If the size of a window or the number of icons in it prevents you from viewing every icon in the window, a **scroll bar** will automatically appear on either the right side or the bottom of the window. This bar allows you to move to the right and left or up and down to see the remaining items in the window. There are three different ways to use the scroll bar. *(See Figure 7.)*

Figure 7

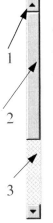

1. Position your mouse on the ▲ button or the ▼ button and click once. Using single clicks enables you to easily read as you go up and down or right and left across the screen. If you click and hold down on either arrow, your view will move very quickly across the screen.

2. To view across the screen, position the mouse pointer over **the button within the bar,** click on it, and hold it while moving it. The size of the button will vary depending on the number of icons in the window. The smaller it is, the more icons there are to scroll through.

3. Within the scroll bar you will see **lightly shaded areas** above and below the scroll button. You can click in these areas to quickly scan back and forth across the monitor screen.

Files and Folders

A file is any document that you have typed in your computer. A **folder** is a container for files. In other words, when you write a letter, you are creating a file. If you want to keep your document in your computer, it must be named and saved. Using the basic saving procedure (which we will discuss later) will save your document onto your computer's hard drive. Once your file is saved onto the hard drive, it can always be retrieved. However, creating specific folders and saving your documents into them allows you to organize the information in your computer in a logical manner. Imagine the difference between piling your typed paper documents into a file cabinet drawer, and organizing your drawer with folders into which you can systematically place your work.

It is easy to tell the difference between file and folder icons. Any icon that is yellow and looks like a folder with a small tab on the top is a folder. Any other icons are files, which may have different shapes and colors. It doesn't matter what they look like—anything that is not a yellow folder is a file. The only exceptions to this would be the descriptive graphic icons you might find in the My Computer window, like your floppy drive, CD ROM drive, or hard drive icons.

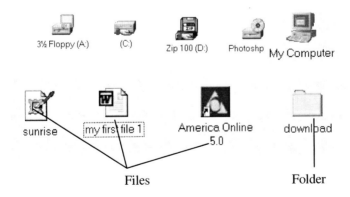

3½ Floppy (A:)   (C:)   Zip 100 (D:)   Photoshp   My Computer

sunrise   my first file 1   America Online 5.0   download

Files   Folder

Exercise I

Part A

1. Place your mouse pointer over the **My Computer icon** on your desktop and double-click on it to open it.

2. Double-click on the **hard drive (C:) icon** to open it. (If you have Windows 95, there will now be two windows on the screen. If you have Windows 98 or 2000, the previous window—My Computer—is going to close automatically and only one window will remain on the screen. To keep the window you are in open while opening the new window, hold down the **Ctrl key** while double-clicking on any folder icon.)

3. Open four additional folders that are in the C: drive window, using this same technique.

4. Arrange the six windows on your screen (i.e., your Desktop) so they cover the entire screen, lined up next to each other in any size and design you choose. There should be no spaces anywhere in between them. Use your window-moving and resizing techniques (from page 39) to do this. *(See the example below.)*

Part B

When you have finished arranging windows on the Desktop, do the following exercise (working with one window at a time):

1. Click on the **Maximize icon.**

2. Click on the **Restore icon.**

3. Click on the **Minimize icon.** (Before minimizing the window, locate it on the Taskbar so that you can recognize it later when you want to restore it.)

4. Look on the **Taskbar** to find the window that you just minimized and click on it to restore it back to the original size.

5. Click on the **Close icon** to close the window.

6. Repeat this process for all of the other open windows on the screen.

Checking Drive Capacity

You can learn the original size of your hard drive and how much storage space is left on it by following these steps:

1. Double-click on the **My Computer icon** if it is not already opened.

2. Move the mouse pointer over the desired drive icon and click on the **right** button. You will see a menu of options.

3. Click the left mouse button once over the **Properties** option to select it. The screen will display the original drive capacity plus the amount of used and free space.

4. To close the window, click on the **Close icon** in the screen's top-right corner or click on the window's **Cancel button.** *(See Figure 8.)*

   Note: To check the capacity of a floppy or CD ROM disk, insert the disk. To check the hard drive, nothing needs to be inserted because the hard disk is built into the hard drive.

Figure 8

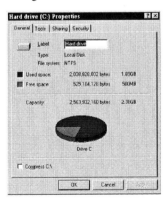

Checking Ram Capacity

As mentioned earlier, RAM is your computer's memory and working space. If you do not have enough RAM when you try to run a program, you will get the **"Insufficient Memory"** error message. It's important to know how much RAM your computer has by performing the following procedure:

1. Double-click on the **My Computer icon** if it is not already open.

2. Double-click on the **Control Panel folder** to open it.

3. Double-click on the **System icon.** (You may need to scroll down in this window to find it.) The **System Properties window** will appear, listing your computer's memory and other information. *(See Figure 9.)*

4. To close the window, click on the **Close icon** in the screen's top-right corner or click on the window's **Cancel button.**

Figure 9

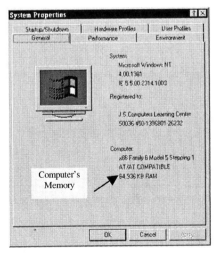

Viewing Icons

When you have opened your hard drive or any other window, you may see many folder and file icons. Your computer will always sort folder icons first, then the file icons. *(See Figure 10.)* You can change the way you view these icons, for different purposes, as follows:

Figure 10

Large Icons

Click on **View** in the Menu bar and click on **Large Icons** to select it. You will see the icons in the window shift to a large size, as shown in Figure 10.

Advantage of Using Large Icons: They are easier to read.

Small Icons

Click on **View** in the Menu bar and click on **Small Icons** to select it. You will see the icons in the window shift to a small size. *(See Figure 11.)*

Figure 11

Advantage of Using Small Icons: This window makes more icons visible at the same time, all sorted horizontally.

List

Click on **View** in the Menu bar and click on **List** to select it. You will see the icons in the window shift to a small size, with all files and then folders in vertical row. *(See Figure 12.)*

Figure 12

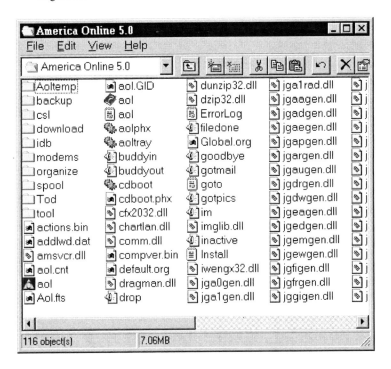

Advantage of Using List: This window presents small icons, and they are all sorted vertically. They might be easier to read when listed in this way.

Details

Click on **View** in the Menu bar and click on **Details** to select it. You will see the icons in the window shift to rows, with a list of details following each icon. *(See Figure 13.)*

Figure 13

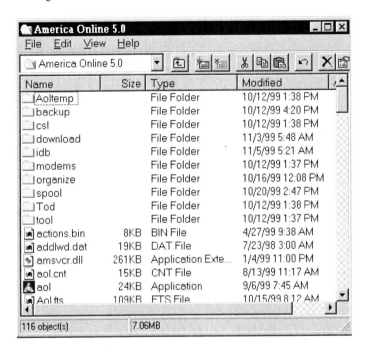

Advantage of Using Details: This window gives details about the size of the item, the date it was last modified, and the type of file it is. These details can help you find a file if, for example, you forget the name of the file but you remember the date you created it. The type of icon for the file indicates what program was used to create it (e.g., a blue *W* means a file was created in Microsoft Word).

Arrange Icons

Click on **View** in the Menu bar and click on **Arrange Icons** to select it. Choose the desired arrangement for sorting. All

file icons can be sorted by name, type, size, and date. *(See Figure 14.)*

Note: *Before using the Arrange Icons feature, first put your icons in a Detail view.*

Figure 14

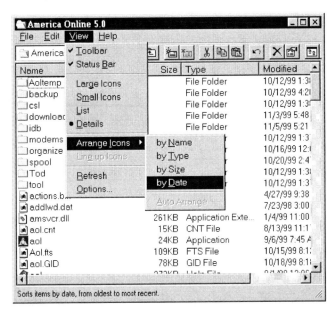

Advantage of Using Arrange Icons: Allows you to arrange and locate items in a variety of ways.

Exercise II

Spend 5–10 minutes practicing each of the above commands. Open and close each window you use.

Section 3
Working with Files and Folders

Creating New Folders

Just as you need to organize your paperwork at home or in your office in a file cabinet with folders on different subjects, you also need to organize the information in your computer. You've already seen that your computer has folders created for the different programs you have installed. You also need to be able to make your own folders and sub-folders for the documents you create. Having a system of folders and sub-folders allows you to easily and logically access all of the information you want to save and retrieve.

For example, you might create a folder for "Insurance Information." Within this **parent folder,** you might want to create a separate **sub-folder** for each type of insurance you have (e.g., car, home, or life). To further organize the contents, you can then categorize these sub-folders by creating within them sub-folders for different years. This type of organizing is very important if you need to separate work-related documents from those pertaining to personal issues. The folders are exactly the same; the "parent" and "sub-" designations are simply used to help you organize them logically.

There are a few ways to create a new folder. You will learn how to perform them all by the end of this book, but we will start with the following procedure:

1. Double-click on the **My Computer icon** on your desktop to open it.

2. Double-click on the **Drive C: icon** to open it.

3. Click on **File** in the Menu bar; a sub-menu will appear.

Figure 15

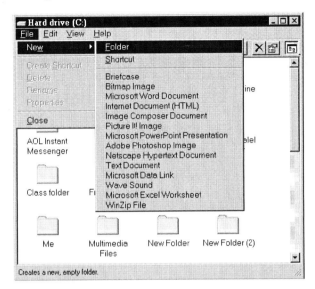

4. Place your mouse pointer on **New** and click to select it. Move your mouse pointer over to the **Folder** selection in the **submenu** that appears, and click on Folder to select it. *(See Figure 15.)*

You will see a **yellow folder icon** appear in the C: Drive window. This will have a title box with highlighted text that says "New Folder." *(See Figure 16 on page 54.)*

5. Type **the desired name** for your folder (e.g., "Susan's Folder") into the title box. You can just type right over highlighted text without deleting it first, or you can click in the middle of text to change of add characters.

Figure 16

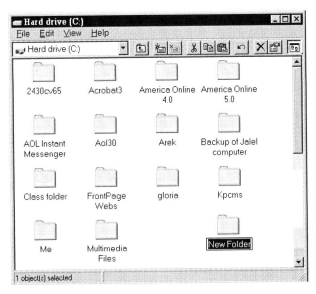

6. Press the **Enter key** located on the right side of the keyboard.

    To make a sub-folder, first open the parent folder you have already created, then repeat the same steps and give the sub-folder a different name for further identification. In other words, follow steps 3–6 inside the parent folder, rather than in the C: Drive window.

Exercise III

Take a piece of paper and categorize a group of activities. For example, you can make a folder for each person who uses the computer. Then, inside this folder, you can create two sub-folders and call them "Personal" and "Work." Then, inside the "Personal" folder, create two more folders and name them "Friends" and "Family." Continue creating new folders and sub-folders until you are comfortable with the procedure.

Renaming Files and Folders

Sometimes you might want to change a file or folder's name; you could have misspelled a name, or you might want a more specific one. To rename a file or folder, do the following:

1. Locate the **icon** of a file or folder that you want to rename.

2. Click once on the **name** of the file or folder icon, and wait a moment. Click on the icon name again, and you will get a **blinking cursor** and **highlighted text.**

3. Type the **new folder's name** over the existing name. If you want to edit the existing name, press any arrow key to remove highlighting and make changes.

4. Click on the **Enter key** when you are finished.

Working with Programs

So far, you have learned how to access your computer's various drives, create folders and files, and work with several elements of the Windows program. The next steps involve opening programs (e.g., word processing) and creating or saving documents.

To open any program, first check to see if there is an icon for it on your desktop screen. If the icon is there, double-click on it. This is a shortcut. To open a program using the usual method, do the following:

1. Click on the **Start button.** *(See Figure 17.)*

2. Move the mouse pointer up to the **Programs option** and a sub-menu will appear.

Figure 17

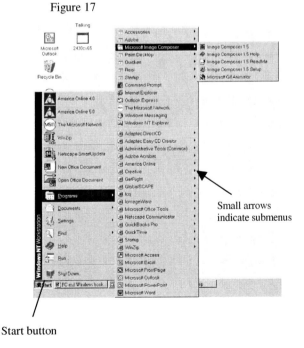

Small arrows indicate submenus

Start button

3. Move the mouse pointer straight across the highlighted bar to the Programs sub-menu, then up or down to select the desired program option. If more sub-menus are available, you may need to move over to them to find your program
4. Click on the desired program to open it.

Exercise IV

Practice opening and closing the **Solitaire game** that is available in most Windows programs. If Solitaire is not in your Windows program, practice the same steps with the **Calculator.**

To play **Solitaire,** select **Start, Program, Accessories, Games,** and **Solitaire.** Open and close Solitaire three times. If you are familiar with the game, play it for a few minutes—it can provide you some good practice using your mouse.

To use the **Calculator,** select **Start, Program, Accessories,** and **Calculator.** The calculator you will see on your screen works just like a real one. Three options are available to you to use this feature. You can use (a) the mouse pointer to work the buttons on the screen, (b) the number buttons just above the letter keys on your keyboard, or (c) the number pad located on the right side of your keyboard (which is easiest if you are using the calculator for a long period of time). Open and close the Calculator three times, and practice working with all three methods.

Creating A Document

Your Windows operating system includes a simple word processing program called **WordPad**. If you do not have any other word processing programs in your computer for typing letters, memos, or other documents (e.g., Microsoft Word or WordPerfect), you can use this program. Use WordPad by following these steps:

1. Click on **Start**, **Programs**, **Accessories**, and **Wordpad.** This will open the WordPad program and a white screen will appear. You will notice a small vertical line blinking at the top-left corner of the screen; this is your cursor. It is like an electronic pen. You cannot type without a cursor and you should always be aware of the location of your cursor, because this is the point at which you will type. *(See Figure 18.)*

Figure 18

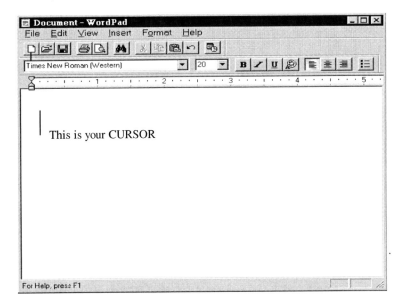

2. Now, type a few paragraphs. Remember: Press the Enter key only when you want to start a new paragraph. Unlike typewriters, computers automatically "wrap" (i.e., continue) typed text onto the next line, so there is no need to press the Enter key when you reach the end of a line. Do not worry about making mistakes as you type—we will learn how to correct them after you finish typing.

3. There are several important keyboard keys that you can use to correct typing mistakes. At the bottom of the keyboard, there is a set of four directional **arrow keys** that

    you can use to move your cursor to any location within the text. You can also use your mouse pointer to do the same thing. When it is within the text area, your mouse pointer will turn into an I-shape. When the I-shape is at the desired area, click once to move the cursor to that place.

    Note: The I-shape alone is not a cursor; you must click your mouse to relocate the cursor to where the I-shape appears.

4. Once you have your cursor next to the text you want to correct, press the **Backspace key** to delete typed information to the left of the cursor. Press the **Delete key** to delete information to the right of the cursor. Once you have deleted your mistakes, you can type in your corrections. *(See the next page for details.)*

Keys Used to Correct Text

Arrow keys

When making corrections, the arrow keys help you to move the cursor only within text. If there is no text, you cannot use the arrow keys.

Note: Blank spaces created by pressing the space bar or the Enter key are considered to be part of the text, so the cursor can move within these spaces.

Enter key

Pressing the Enter key creates a new line just below the position of the cursor. If the cursor is in the middle of a line when you press the Enter key, you will move the rest of the text on the line to the one below it and be left with half a blank line. If your mouse pointer is at the beginning or end of a line and you press the Enter key, you will create a completely blank line.

Backspace

Pressing the backspace key deletes to the **left** of the cursor.

Delete key

Pressing the Delete key deletes to the **right** of the cursor.

Keyboard Shortcuts to Move the Cursor Around Your Document

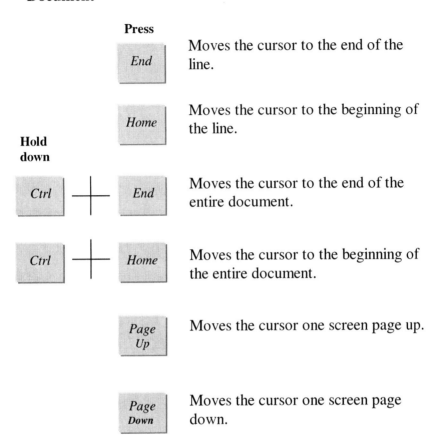

Press

End — Moves the cursor to the end of the line.

Home — Moves the cursor to the beginning of the line.

Hold down

Ctrl + End — Moves the cursor to the end of the entire document.

Ctrl + Home — Moves the cursor to the beginning of the entire document.

Page Up — Moves the cursor one screen page up.

Page Down — Moves the cursor one screen page down.

Exercise V

Use the above steps to type and correct several text paragraphs. You have now created a document (i.e., a file). We will now learn how to save the document in your computer.

Saving Files

You must know how to save a file in order to keep your information in the computer. Therefore, this is a very important step to learn. No matter what you create on your computer or what program you use, you must save a file in order to be able to retrieve it. It is important to save any document as soon as you begin working on it. While you are working on it, you should routinely save every five minutes or so by using the following steps:

1. Click on **File** in the Menu bar above your document. You will see a menu with two save options, **Save** and **Save As.**

   Save As is used the first time you save a file; this is when you want to name it and name the location for saving it (e.g., the folder you want to save the file into). To save changes made to the file after naming it, use **Save.**

2. Click on **Save As.** A **dialog box** will appear. Here, you will name your file and tell the computer where to save it. *(See Figure 19 on page 63.)*

3. Type in **the name you would like to use for the file**—one that you will recognize later on—in the box called **File name.** You will see this box near the bottom of the Save As dialog box. It might be blank inside, or there might be highlighted text that gives the first few words of your document or simply says "Document." Your typed-in name will automatically replace any highlighted words.

   Note: Never use these punctuation marks as part of your file name: | \ ? : * " < >
   These are commands for the computer; using them in the file name will give you an error message.

Figure 19

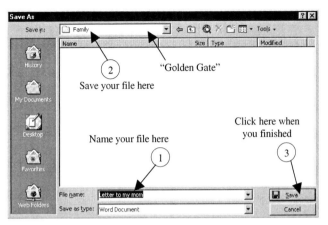

"Golden Gate"

Save your file here

Name your file here

Click here when you finished

4. **Locate the place into which you want to save your file.** At the top of the Save As dialog box you will see a small box called Save in. This is where you will tell the computer the desired location for your file. I call this area the **"Golden Gate"** because it is so important to know where you are saving your files. At the right side of this box, there is a selection arrow. Click on it, and a list of options will appear; these tell you where you can save your file. You will usually see the icons and names appear for your Desktop, My Computer, all your drives, and any folders that are on your Desktop. The name of the location you click on will appear in the Save in box; this location is where your file will be saved.

You can have access to any place in your hard drive or floppy drive to save your file. For example, let's say you want to save your file inside a folder that you have already created, named "Friends." The "Friends" folder you created is located inside the "Personal" folder. The "Personal" folder is inside the folder under your name, which is located in your hard drive. If the folder (in this

case, "Friends") is not visible in the window below the "Golden Gate" box, use the following steps to find it:

A. Click on the selection arrow (to the right of the **Save in box (i.e., the "Golden Gate")**. A drop-down menu will appear.

B. Select **Drive C** (if you are not already in it), which is at the top of the menu. Look for the folder titled with your name. (If you cannot see it, use the scroll bar to find it.)

C. Double-click on your named folder to open it. This will move the name of your folder to the top, into the Save in box; the folder's contents will be displayed underneath.

D. Double-click on the "Personal" folder, and do the same on the "Friends" folder that will be displayed. At this point, you should see the "Friends" folder name at the top of the Save in box. If you click on the Save button, your file is going to be saved in that folder.

5. Click on the **Save button** in the bottom-right corner of the dialog box to complete the process. Following the above steps, you have named your file and told the computer where to save it.

Opening Existing Files

Once you have opened your program, it is easy to open an existing file by doing the following:

1. Click on **File** in the Menu bar.

2. Click on **Open.** A dialog box will appear. *(See Figure 20.)*

3. If you do not see the folder that your file is saved in, and you are not already in Drive C, go to the **Look In** box (at the top of the dialog box). Use the selection arrow at the immediate right to select the location of your file. For example, if a file is in a folder that is located in Drive C, first select Drive C and then **double-click on the desired folder** from the drive's contents displayed in the box.

Note: The computer normally displays the last folder opened in the "Look in" box. So, if you are retrieving the same file a second time, it might already be displayed.

Figure 20

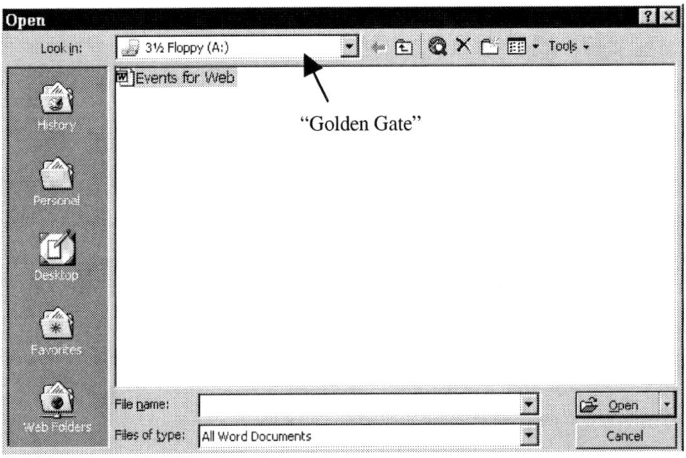

4. Double-click on **your file name** to open.

Opening Files From Floppy Disk

When opening a file from a floppy disk, follow the same procedures as above. However, first be sure that your floppy disk is in the floppy drive. When you select the Look in option from the "Golden Gate," click on Drive A (i.e., the floppy drive) and then open your file.

Exercise VI

Create several files and save them into different folders that you have already created. Then, open each file one at a time, type a few words in each, and save the changes.

As you finish working on each file, close the program and repeat the steps.

Section 4
Working Between Files

Copying Files Between Hard Drive and Floppy Drive

Copying From Hard Drive To Floppy Drive

Even if you have followed the saving procedures outlined above, files and folders in your hard drive are not 100% safe from being lost. If, for any reason, your hard drive "crashes" (i.e., is physically damaged), you can lose everything that you have saved on it. Therefore, it is extremely important to copy any document on your hard drive that you want to keep onto a floppy disk (or onto a zip disk if you have a zip drive).

You can also copy from a floppy disk onto your hard drive if, for example, someone gives you a disk with information on it that you would like to have in your computer. Let's begin with copying from the hard drive to the floppy or zip drives.

1. Place your floppy disk in the floppy drive or zip disk in the zip drive. From your desktop, double-click on the **My Computer icon** to open it.

2. Double-click on **Drive C** to open it.

   Note: When using Windows 95, the parent (e.g., "My Computer") window will remain open when you open a window within it. If you are using Windows 98, you must hold down the Ctrl key when you double-click to open a window, or the parent window will automatically close.

3. Locate the file or folder that you want to copy. You must be able to see both the floppy drive (i.e., Drive A) icon in the "My Computer" window and the icon for the item you want to copy. You might have to move or adjust the size of your windows to do this.

4. Click on the icon of the file or folder you want to copy and **hold the mouse button down** with your finger **while you drag it** over the floppy drive icon. *(See Figure 21.)* When you see the icon become highlighted, let go of the button. To make sure the copying has occurred, you can double-click over the floppy drive icon to open the floppy drive window. You should see the new file icon inside the window.

Figure 21

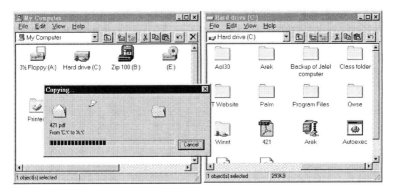

Copying From Floppy Drive To Hard Drive

Copying a file or folder from the floppy drive to the hard drive uses the same procedures as above, but you are going from Drive A to Drive C, instead of the other way around.

1. Make sure that your floppy disk is in the floppy drive. Double-click on the **My Computer icon** on your desktop to open it.

2. Double-click on the **Drive A** icon to open the **floppy drive window**. The icon for the folder or file you wish to copy should appear. If the file is inside a folder, you must open the folder first with a double-click to get to the file icon.

3. Go back to the **My Computer window** and open **Drive C**. To copy into a particular folder, you must be able to see its icon. (You may have to scroll through this window to find it.) At this point, you must be able to see the icon in Drive A that you want to copy and the location in Drive C where you want to place it.

4. Move your mouse pointer over the file icon in the Drive A window from which you want to copy. Click and **hold down the mouse button while you drag the icon, placing it over the folder into which you want it copied.** When the folder becomes highlighted, release the button. To confirm that copying occurred, open the folder you copied into—you should see the new file icon there.

Moving Files

You can move files and folders within a single drive. This is a quick way to place a file into an existing folder. You can also move a folder into another folder. For example, if you move Folder X into Folder Y, Folder X will become a sub-folder of Folder Y. To organize your folder, follow these steps:

1. Make sure both folder or file icons—the one you are moving <u>and</u> the one into which you will move—are visible on your screen.

2. Click on **the icon you want to move.** Hold down your mouse button and drag the icon over the icon into which you are moving. When the folder is highlighted, release.

3. You can follow the same steps within a folder by moving file icons into folder icons.

   Note: If you click and drag files or folders between drives, you are <u>copying</u>. If you click and drag within the same drive, you are <u>moving.</u>

Deleting Files Or Folders

On your Desktop screen is an icon called **"Recycle Bin."** The Recycle Bin is used to delete files or folders; this process has two parts. The first part is used to put files or folders into the Recycle Bin, from which they are still retrievable. The second part is used to empty the Recycle Bin, and permanently deletes whatever is in it. To delete, do the following:

1. Make sure that both the **Recycle Bin icon** and the icon for **the item you want to delete** are visible on your screen.

2. Click on the **file or folder you are deleting**, hold down the mouse button and **drag the icon over the Recycle Bin icon.** Once the Recycle bin becomes highlighted, release the mouse pointer. At this point, you have moved the item into the recycle bin, but you can still retrieve it. To complete the deleting procedure, continue with the following steps. *(See Figure 22.)*

Figure 22

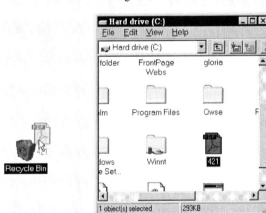

3. Double-click on the **Recycle Bin icon** to open it.

4. Click on **File** in the Menu bar and click once on **Empty Recycle Bin** to select it. *(See Figure 23 on page 73.)*

Figure 23

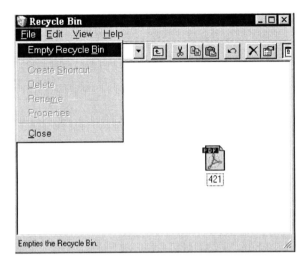

5. The computer will ask if you are sure you want to delete this. Click on **"Yes"** to confirm. *(See Figure 24.)*

Figure 24

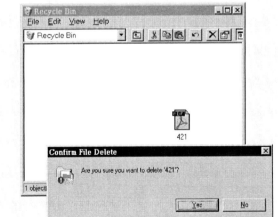

6. Click on the **Close button** to close the Recycle Bin window.

Note 1: *If, after dragging a file or folder into the recycle bin, you decide you do not want to delete it, open the Recycle Bin window and click on the desired file or folder. Drag it over to the Desktop release the mouse pointer button.*

Note 2: *The Recycle Bin cannot hold files or folders from a floppy disk, so the computer will ask you to empty the bin as soon as you place an item in it.*

Note 3: *If you have Windows 95 and you place a folder that has files in it into the Recycle Bin, the folder will automatically be permanently deleted. However, its files will remain in the Recycle Bin until you empty it.*

Finding Files Or Folders

If you forget where you saved a file, or even if you forget its exact name, you can use the **Find command** in the Windows program to find the file for you. To do this, use the following steps:

1. Click on the **Start button.**

2. Move your mouse pointer to the **Find option;** a sub-menu will appear.

3. Move your mouse pointer to the **Files or Folders option** on the sub-menu and click once; a dialog box will appear.

4. Type the name of the item you are looking for into the box marked **Named.**

5. Click on the **Find Now button.** *(See Figure 25.)*

Figure 25

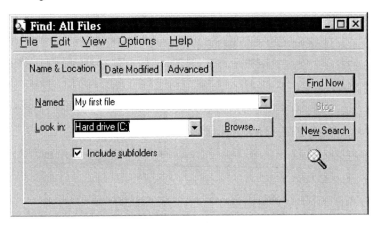

Note: If the computer does not find what you are looking for, try again using fewer letters or words; this gives the computer more options to search through. For example, if you are looking for a file named "Lesson I Notes" and it is not found, try typing just the word "Lesson," which broadens out the search. The computer might then find more matches (e.g., "Lesson I," "Lesson II", "Computer Lesson," etc.).

If this does not find the file, you can further broaden out the search by having Windows *look for the letters you have typed, even if they are just a few letters from the complete file name. If, continuing with our example, you type just the letters "son," the computer will offer you all matches that contain what you have typed. In other words, the computer might also find files like "Peterson" or "Sonic Devices" or even "Sony."*

6. Windows will display the results of its search and you can look for your file. You might have to use the scroll arrows provided if there are many choices. When you find your file, you will see that the columns next to it give you its location, size, and type. You can double-click on the file or folder icon to open it, or you can click on it and drag it onto your Desktop.

Section 5
Working with Microsoft Explore

Microsoft Explore

Up to this point, we have looked at the basics of organizing the files or folders in your computer. You now know more about your computer's drives, files, and folders, as well as ways to save and retrieve your documents. Let's look at a different, perhaps easier, way to deal with your filing system—by using the Microsoft Explore function. To access Explore, follow these steps:

1. Position your mouse pointer over the **Start button** and click once on the **right mouse button.** In Windows, a right click will always display a menu of options.

2. Click on **Explore.** You will see a window that is divided into two parts. If you are already familiar with the older Window 3.1 version, you will notice a similarity to that version's "File Manager." *(See Figure 26.)*

Figure 26

3. On the left side of your screen, under "All Folders," is a list of everything contained in your computer, starting from the top with your Desktop icon. The next items will be indented in a hierarchical pattern that shows where they are contained. *(See Figure 27.)* For example, indented just to the right under Desktop, you will see My Computer, because you will find My Computer on your Desktop.

4. Use the **scroll bars** to scroll up and down the list. If an item is indented, it means that it is contained within the item above it. The next indented items below My Computer will be the icons for the drives the computer contains. Indented just to the right under Drive C, you will see icons for all of the folders and sub-folders that are stored there.

Figure 27

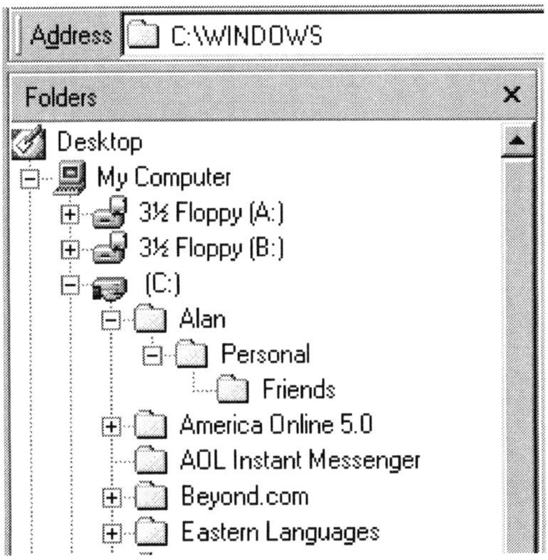

If you see a plus sign (+) to the left of an icon, it means there are more icons or folders contained inside that folder. when you click on the plus sign, you will see the list of items that are stored there. If you see a minus sign (-) to the left of an icon, it means that folder is open; below the icon, indented, will be a list of all items contained in that folder.

If you click on the minus sign, you will close that icon and it will no longer show its contents on the screen. If there is no sign to the left of an icon, then there are no sub-folders in that folder. Click on any icon on the left side of the screen to see its contents; these will then be displayed on the right side of the divided screen. Also, after doing this, you will see the name of the icon in the small box above the **All Folders List.**

You can open any folder or file from the Explore screen. For example, you might want to open File X, which is in Folder Y, and this folder is contained in Drive C. Look for Folder Y on the left side of the folder list and click on it. Now Folder Y will be selected on the left side and all its contents will be displayed on the right side. Look for File X and double-click on it to open it.

Exercise VII

Spend 5–10 minutes practicing opening and closing the icons on the left side of your screen, clicking on the plus and minus signs as you do this. Notice the changes that appear on the right side of your screen as you follow these steps.

What Can We Do in Explore?
Everything that we have learned to do so far we can also do in
Explore by using the procedures that follow below. This
includes creating folders; copying, deleting, and finding files;
viewing and sorting files, etc.

Making New Folders

1. Click on the **parent folder** (i.e., the one that will hold your
   new folder.)

2. Click on **File** in the Menu bar and select **New.** Move your
   mouse over to the sub-menu and click once on **Folder.**
   (See Figure 28.)

3. Type the desired name **over the highlighted text.**

4. Press the **Enter key.**

Figure 28

Copying Files and Folders

Copying from Floppy Drive to Hard Drive

1. Click on the **floppy drive icon** (normally found on the top-left side of the screen) to see its contents on the right side of screen.

2. If you see your file you want to copy on the right side, but you cannot see the folder that you want to copy to on the left side, use your scroll bar to scroll up and down until you find it. Then, click on the file you're copying and drag it **over the folder into which you want to copy.** When this folder is highlighted, release the mouse pointer and wait for Windows to complete the copying operations.

Copying from Hard Drive to Floppy Drive

1. Locate the file that you want to copy.

2. Drag your file icon **over the floppy drive icon** and release the mouse pointer.

Moving Files or Folders
As mentioned before, if you click and drag between files and folders within a drive, you are moving, not copying them. Knowing how to move your files and folders helps you to organize your filing system. If you have not organized your files and folders, use this helpful procedure to do so.

Deleting Files

To delete files and folders from the Explore screen, do the following:

1. Click the **right** button over the desired file or folder.

2. Click on the **Delete** option. *(See Figure 29.)*

3. Click on **Yes** to confirm.

4. Double-click on the **Recycle Bin** icon to open it.

5. Click on **File** in the Menu bar and select **Empty Recycle Bin.**

6. Click on **Yes** to confirm (but be sure you want to delete it, because this is the last chance you have to change your mind before it is permanently deleted).

Figure 29

Renaming Files or Folders

1. Click the **right button** over the desired icon.

2. Click on **Rename.** You will see highlighted text and a blinking cursor.

3. Simply **type the new name** or use **the arrow keys** to remove highlighting, and then make changes to existing name.

4. Press the **Enter key** when you are finished.

Viewing and Sorting Files

As discussed earlier, if you click on a folder on the left side of the Explore screen and you see icons on the right side, you can sort them by using the View command in the Menu bar and selecting your desired option. (Refer to the section on "Viewing Icons" on page 49.)

Tips To Avoid Trouble...

...Using Me, Your Mouse!

➢ Treat me, your mouse, like a <u>loaded gun</u>: always watch where my on-screen pointer is, where it is moving to, and what you click on. If you click accidentally, stop to see what happened (just as you would if you'd accidentally fired a gun). When looking at the screen, don't just stare in only one spot. Look all over the screen to see if there are any changes or if any message appears. If you don't do this, you might get into a situation you don't want to be in.

➢ When you click on me, just **click <u>lightly</u> and release**. It just takes a light finger-touch to make me work!

➢ When you use me to move the cursor to different positions in a document, move the cursor to where you want it, <u>stop</u>, before you click. <u>Don't</u> make even small movements with me <u>while you are clicking my button</u>. If you do, you'll see a small bar where your cursor should be...and you might think the cursor has disappeared.

Solution: Click my button somewhere in the text, or press one of the arrow keys to get to either side of the small bar. There you will see your cursor. Easy!

➢ When using me to move your mouse pointer within text, move me <u>without</u> holding my button down, or you'll be highlighting text instead of moving my pointer. This is similar to getting the small bar (mentioned above), but you might have entire text blocks highlighted.

Solution: Click me again or press an arrow key to get to either side of the highlighted text. There's your cursor!

➢ Always be very careful when your mouse pointer is <u>in a list</u> of files or folders. **Never <u>click as you move me</u> up or down a list and <u>release my button</u>!** You might accidentally move a file or folder into another one and misplace files…and sometime may even permanently ruin some programs.

Solution: If this occurs, stop immediately to see what has happened. Don't keep moving or clicking, because you can get into even more trouble and not realize it. The following steps can help you to solve the problem:

1. If you **know which file or folder you moved the other file or folder into**, open that folder and drag the icon of that file or folder to the original place.

2. If you see that you just lost the file or folder your mouse pointer was on, and you **don't know where to look for it but you do know its name** or some information of that file or folder, use the **Find command** to locate it. *(See page 75.)*

3. If you **don't even know that**, then you may be in greater difficulty, because the only solution is to open all the folders that you have in your hard drive to find if any program folder has been misplaced in a different folder. After you find it, just drag the file or folder back to hard drive window.

Tips To Avoid Trouble...

 ...Using Me, Your Keyboard!

➤ Press my keys <u>gently</u> when making keystrokes. You only need to touch lightly enough to type the letters and numbers. Applying more pressure on my keys will make characters rrrrrrepeat.

➤ The <u>only keys</u> you can hold down without repeating characters are the **Shift key** and the **Ctrl key** (and, in a few cases, the **Alt key**). All of my other keys work on a fast touch-and-release basis.

➤ Before you type anything with me, first <u>look at the screen</u>. If your cursor is not visible within a document, you might be typing in computer commands that you don't really want the computer to perform.

Tips To Get Out Of Trouble

Computer Freeze-Ups

If your computer freezes up and your keyboard or your mouse suddenly stop working, there are steps you can take.

a) If your keyboard works and your mouse doesn't work, you can escape from the frozen program by doing the following:

Hold down the **Ctrl key** plus the **Alt key** with one hand, and lightly press the **Delete key** with the other hand. When the **Close Program box** appears, your only option is to press the **Enter key** to accept the **End Task command.** (NOTE: You will lose any information or changes that were added since you last saved, which is why it is VERY important to keep saving any file every 5 minutes or so as you work on it.) By following these steps (i.e., ending the current task), the computer closes the program you are having trouble with, and returns you to your Desktop.

b) If neither your keyboard nor your mouse works, simply turn off the computer by using its On/Off button, wait about 10 seconds, and turn the computer back on.

c) If the above steps a) and b) do not solve the problem, call a technician and request professional assistance.

"Invalid system disk" or "Non-system disk"

When you turn your computer on, if your computer gives you the message **"Invalid system disk"** or **"Non-system disk"** (rather than first showing you the Windows screen), it means that you have a floppy disk inserted that your computer is trying to read. Your computer cannot read a floppy disk until it first opens the Windows program.

Solution: Just remove the floppy disk and press any key on your keyboard.

➤ Can't locate the Taskbar

If you can't find the taskbar at the bottom of the screen where it usually belongs, you can find it in a different place on the screen (e.g., the side or top). This means that you have accidentally positioned your mouse over the task bar and moved it to another part of the screen.

Solution: Position the mouse pointer on a spot on the task bar where there are no file or folder buttons visible. Then, drag the pointer toward the screen bottom, and let go. The task bar should reappear at the bottom of the screen.

➤ The Taskbar is too wide

If you notice that your taskbar is too wide and covers half of your desktop, this means that you accidentally changed the size of your taskbar.

Solution: Position the mouse pointer on the edge of the taskbar. When you get a double arrow, click and drag the edge of the taskbar down to get it to its original size.

Index